CAFFEINE
+
CHARACTER

Steven Case

THE
PILGRIM
PRESS
Cleveland

This book is dedicated to the youth of the
Windermere Union Church, United Church of Christ.
They are, without a doubt, the finest group of young people that
I have ever worked with. It is my honor to be called
their minister.

The Pilgrim Press, 700 Prospect Avenue, Cleveland, Ohio 44115-1100
thepilgrimpress.com
© 2008 by Steven Case

Scripture quotations, unless otherwise noted, are from the New
Revised Standard Version of the Bible, © 1989 by the Division of
Christian Education of the National Council of Churches of Christ in
the United States of America and are used by permission. Changes
have been made for inclusivity.

13   12   11   10   09   08   5   4   3   2   1

Library of Congress Cataloging-in-Publication Data

Case, Steve L., 1964-
 Caffeine and character / Steven Case.
    p. cm.
 ISBN-13: 978-0-8298-1806-2 (alk. paper)
 1. Youth--Religious life. 2. Devotional exercises. I. Title.
 BV4531.3.C366 2008
 242'.63--dc22

                           2008014346

CONTENTS

Exploration 1: Passing Go 4

Exploration 2: Who's in Charge Here? 8

Exploration 3: Soda-Popularity 12

Exploration 4: Leggo My Ego 16

Exploration 5: I've Got the Joy, Joy, Joy 20

Exploration 6: Signature of Parent or Guardian 24

Exploration 7: I Am What I Am 28

Exploration 8: Model Behavior 32

Exploration 9: Gooooooaaaaallll! 36

Exploration 10: Des-ta-neee, Des-ta-neee

—No Escaping That for Me 42

Exploration 11: Whoooo Are You? Who? Who? 46

Exploration 12: From the Inside Out 50

Exploration 13: Are You Out of Your Mind? 54

Exploration 14: Wabbit Season! Duck Season! 58

Exploration 15: Hindsight 20/20 62

Exploration 16: Take Me 66

Exploration 17: Cannonball!!!! 70

Exploration 18: Find Out What it Means to Me 74

Afterword: How to Use This Book 79

PASSING GO

THEME: YOU

ORDER HERE

We have to start here. This is big idea number one. You have to get this or the rest of the book will not do you any good. *You are who you are because that is who you have chosen to be.* Got that? You are who you are because that is who you have chosen to be. Who you are is not because your mom smokes, your dad drinks too much coffee, your brother is better looking, or your sister got better grades. You are who you are because that is who you have chosen to be. (With thanks to C. McNair Wilson)

START THINKING

Choose one. I'd rather be...

- In the city / In the country
- In a corner office / Plowing the fields on my tractor
- Watching "Rugrats" / Watching "Dogma"
- A plain bagel / A chocolate sugar puck with sprinkles
- The hammer / The nail
- Here / Someplace else
- Writing / Reading
- Cooking / Eating
- Driving / Riding
- Student / Teacher

TABLE NOTES

Using a blank page in your journal or the back of a place mat or napkin...

- Come up with five words that I think other people use to describe me.
- Put an **X** in any of the five words that aren't even close to describing me.
- Write three words that I use to describe myself (These must be positive and affirming words that have nothing to do with physical description. If that's all you can think of, think a little longer.)
- The one thing I do that, while I'm doing it, makes me feel the most alive.

Fill in the blank: I feel I am in the presence of the Creator God when I am:

SCRIPTURE MENU

Have someone look up the verses, and ask the questions aloud.

1 Corinthians 3:16 (NIV)

Don't you know that you yourselves are God's temple and that God's Spirit lives in you?

Putting all addictions aside (drugs, alcohol, grease, caffeine, sugar), what if this verse is describing the mental, spiritual, and emotional rather than the physical?

Most of us could "fix" the physical things. But how do we fix ourselves in nonphysical ways to become "temples"?

Ephesians 2:19 (MsgB)

That's plain enough, isn't it? You're no longer wandering exiles. This new world of faith is now your home country. You're no longer strangers or outsiders. You belong here, with as much right to the name "Christian" as anyone. God is building a home. God is using us all—regardless of how we got here—in what God is building.

Think of the Kingdom not as a place but as a realm, a new world, or a lifestyle where everyone looks out for one another. How does that change this verse? How do we Christians expand this new world?

Galatians 3:28 (MsgB)

In Christ's family there can be no division into Jew and non-Jew, slave and free, male and female. Among us, you are all equal. That is, we are all in a common relationship with Jesus Christ.

Why do some religions seem like they are putting conditions on what is unconditional?

Jesus was all about taking down the walls. And yet, in Christ's name, we put them back up again. Where is our responsibility in setting boundaries for the "new world"? Should there be any?

TAKE HOME BAG

Read Psalm 139.
Read the psalm several times. Break it down into sentences if that helps. Do whatever it takes to understand it.

TIP

The God who dreamt the universe into reality, the God who put the stars in place, the God who made angels and ants and volcanoes and bananas...that God, the ever-expanding ever-loving ever-creating creator of the universe, made *you* and you are God's favorite creation.

WHO'S IN CHARGE HERE?

Theme: AUTHORITY

Order Here

When you were small, there was someone whose purpose in life was to look after your well being. If you were hungry, they fed you. If you were cold, the person warmed you. She or he filled out your forms, drove you around, and kicked your butt when you needed it. That changes. You may be living in your parent's house, but now "the authority" is yours. You can choose to break curfew or not. You can choose to study or not. However, you have to live with the consequences of those choices. It's time to choose whom you are going to follow.

Start Thinking

Choose one.

- I'd rather work for a man / woman.
- I'd rather be the boss of someone older than I / someone younger than I.
- I find leadership easy / difficult.
- I'd rather hang out with my boss after work / see my boss only during working hours.
- I can make up my mind about the menu easily / with great difficulty.
- I'd rather order the same thing that I know is good every time /

see what looks good when I get there.

- Authority and respect must be earned / given.
- To get the best work out of a staff made up of high school students, a good manager must encourage and be patient / crack the whip and say, "Suck it up."
- I am more likely to wear a button with "Question Authority" on it / a smiley face on it.

TABLE NOTES

Use a blank page or the back of a place mat or napkin...

- Pick out two or three items from the menu that you think somehow symbolize your personal idea of what "authority" is, and say why.
- List three ways your server has "authority" over you.
- Make a list of five things that you are completely in charge of every day.

Jesus was willing to wrap a towel around his waist and wash the disciples' feet. Jesus said that if you want to be served you have to be willing to serve. What do you think he meant?

SCRIPTURE MENU

Look up one or more of the sets of verses, and respond to the discussion suggestions that follow.

Read Proverbs 18:13–17.

Proverbs is one of those great books that teach us how to get through life, the here and now. After you read the verses, think of places you could apply them in your daily routine.

These verses sound like perfectly acceptable advice you might hear from a friend who's just listened to your problems. What does that suggest about the people for whom this book was originally written?

Much of the book of Proverbs was written as a letter from a father to a son. What do these verses seem to say about how to be a "grown-up"?

Mark 2:23–28

23One sabbath he was going through the grainfields; and as they made their way his disciples began to pluck heads of grain. 24The Pharisees said to him, "Look, why are they doing what is not lawful on the sabbath?" 25And he said to them, "Have you never read what David did when he and his companions were hungry and in need of food? 26He entered the house of God, when Abiathar was high priest, and ate the bread of the Presence, which it is not lawful for any but the priests to eat, and he gave some to his companions." 27Then he said to them, "The sabbath was made for humankind, and not humankind for the sabbath; 28so the Son of Man is lord even of the sabbath."

What does "the sabbath was made for humankind" mean?

Can you think of an example of how we give more authority to "religion" than to "faith"?

What is the purpose of ritual? How does it help us connect to one another and to something larger?

Read Romans 13:1–6 (NRSV).

If experience is the best teacher, how does it affect authority?

Badges, cop lights, and IRS vouchers are symbols of authority. What others can you think of? Is a cross a symbol of authority?

How good are you at "authority"? If you have ever managed a group of people, what was it like?

Do you think God "ordained" our current leaders to be in place? If you think not, what if they agreed with you?

Have you ever seen a "Question Authority" button? When should authority be questioned? What does the button say about the person who is wearing it?

Colossians 2:23 (NIV)
Such regulations indeed have an appearance of wisdom, with their self-imposed worship, their false humility and their harsh treatment of the body, but they lack any value in restraining sensual indulgence.

What does "Let go and let God" mean?

If God is the ultimate authority, why is it so hard to submit to that?

Is it possible to be fired by God?

TABLE NOTES

Use a blank sheet in your journal or the back of a place mat or napkin...

- Make a list of people you know who are in "authority" positions.
- Make a list of people to whom you give authority over you whether or not they have that position.
- Draw a button or bumper sticker that reads: "_____ Authority." Fill in the blank based on what you feel in your own life. Live tomorrow as if you are really wearing the button.

_____ AUTHORITY

TAKE HOME BAG

Read 1 Peter 3:15.
Search your local newspaper and clip out a headline or comic that shows someone who is living his/her authority. Use it as a bookmark in this book.

TIP

The best way to question authority is not with your mouth but with your actions. The same holds true when you want to "show" your authority.

SODA-POPULARITY

THEME: BEING POPULAR

ORDER HERE

You know those monster movies where the "creature" starts off small and eventually consumes a city? Popularity can be like that. We begin to worry more about form than function. We'd rather wear the trendy items and be uncomfortable than wear something that will let us breathe but will bring eye rolls from the cool kids' lunch table. There are no superheroes in the Bible. All the great heroes that our Sunday school papers used to depict as HEROES were really flawed screw-ups who had good press agents. Popularity is like that glass of soda on the counter. If you don't pay attention, it will go flat on you.

START THINKING

Choose one. I'd rather...

- Sit at the cool kids' lunch table / Sit with the band geeks.
- Wear jeans with no label / Wear jeans with a designer's name on the back pocket.
- Be Paris Hilton, heiress / Be Myron Hilton, accountant.
- Order what everyone else is having at a party / Order something I like even if it isn't considered cool.
- Be the tree / Be the ornament on the tree.
- Have a cup of coffee at a Starbucks. / Have a cup of coffee at a 7/11.

TABLE NOTES

Use a blank page or the back of a place mat or napkin...

- Write down the five most popular clothing labels, bands, or technologies that "everyone" likes or is using.
- Draw the "chest symbol" for a superhero called Ordinary Person.
- Write down and complete this formula:

  _____ + _____ – _____ = Popularity.

- Write down the name of the person you know who is the most comfortable in his/her own skin.
- Write down these words: truth, faith, love. Now write down one way each of these is the "money" that buys popularity. (In other words, what do you "give up" of these three in order to be popular?)
- The group Superchick sings about popularity as a "monster that I feed." Draw a quick sketch of the monster.

SCRIPTURE MENU

Look up one or more of the sets of verses, and respond to the discussion suggestions that follow.

1 Corinthians 1:26-31

26Consider your own call, brothers and sisters: not many of you were wise by human standards, not many were powerful, not many were of noble birth. 27But God chose what is foolish in the world to shame the wise; God chose what is weak in the world to shame the strong; 28God chose what is low and despised in the world, things that are not, to reduce to nothing things that are, 29so that no one might boast in the presence of God. 30He is the source of your life in Christ Jesus, who became for us wisdom from God, and righteousness and sanctification and redemption, 31in order that, as it is written, "Let the one who boasts, boast in the Lord."

Is bragging different if you can back it up? How?

Luke 6:26 (NRSV)

"Woe to you when all speak well of you, for that is what their ancestors did to the false prophets."

How much of popularity is just about getting your butt kissed?

Why do celebrity endorsements work?

Romans 12:1 (NRSV)

I appeal to you therefore, brothers and sisters, by the mercies of God, to present your bodies as a living sacrifice, holy and acceptable to God, which is your spiritual worship.

Paul seems to say that to offer yourself as an example of what God wants is like worship. How so?

What does this verse say about popularity?

TAKE HOME BAG

Go home and read Romans 12:2.
Peruse the newspaper or watch TV for an hour.
Write down all the ads that seem to say, "You'd
be popular if only you would use our product."

TIP

Name the winner of last year's...

Oscars
Superbowl
Homecoming
Grammy Awards
Tony Awards
World Series

Did you have to stop and think about it?

LEGGO MY EGO

THEME: EGO

ORDER HERE

Remember Daffy Duck and Pepé Le Pew? Their egos could drive the conflict for an entire episode. There is a line between self-confidence and ego. Self-confidence occurs when you can back it up. Ego occurs when you expect everyone else to.

START THINKING

Choose one. I am...

- Fruit Loops™ / Corn Flakes.
- Old Navy / Sears.
- Coffee / Double Frappa Dappa Cino.
- the Happy Meal™ / the free toy.
- Nike / Converse.

TABLE NOTES

In the space below or the back of a place mat or napkin...

- Draw a dot on your paper. This is you.
- Draw a circle around the dot to represent the size of your ego. (The larger the circle, the larger the ego.) Be honest with yourself here.
- Draw a circle around the dot to represent what your friends would say your ego size is.

How do self-confidence and ego differ?

SCRIPTURE MENU

Have someone look up the verses, and ask the questions aloud.

Read Proverbs 6:16–17.
Pride is on God's list of bad behavior.

Read Proverbs 11:2.
An over-abundance of ego can lead to problems.

Read Proverbs 13:10.
Ego equals argument.

Read Proverbs 16:5.
Ego will end badly, part 1.

Read Proverbs 18:12.
Ego will end badly, part 2.

Read Proverbs 29:23.
Ego will end badly, part 3.

TAKE HOME BAG

Read 1 Corinthians 5:6.
To what does the verse compare arrogance?
Make a list of five other things that would work
as a comparison.

_____

_____

_____

_____

_____

_____

_____

_____

Read 1 Thessalonians 5:14.

Write down an example or a specific behavior for each of the actions listed in this.

TIP

Even if you are the coolest kid in the school, you are allowed to shut up about it once in a while.

I'VE GOT THE JOY, JOY, JOY

Theme: INNER JOY

ORDER HERE

One theme comes up over and over again in the Bible: God's joy is for everyone. Jesus constantly defies the accepted norms about who he can and can't eat lunch with. The book of Acts talks about the perfect community where everyone is accepted for who they are. The people who get in the most trouble with God (including some of God's main people) are the ones who try to lay down the rules about who gets in and who doesn't. If this big idea is so important to God, if God loves you that much—"just a little lower than God and a little above God's angels"—why are you so hard on yourself and on others?

START THINKING

True or False?

- Some people are just born lucky.
- Some people get all of life's good things handed to them on a silver platter.
- God smiles on some people and not on others.
- If a parking spot opens right in front of the mall, it's because God is rewarding me.

- The Bible is a rulebook that nobody can ever really live up to.
- God has a list.
- If you are feeling happy, it means something bad is just around the corner.
- If you are stuck at the bottom of a well, shut up and enjoy the quiet for a change.
- Vanilla is not a flavor.

TABLE NOTES

Use a blank page or the back of a place mat or napkin...

1. Place a dot on the edge of your paper. (This is you.)
2. Draw a circle on the opposite edge. (This is God.)
3. Connect these two dots with a line. Now place an **X** on the line to represent where you think your relationship with God is.

Look at the menu. Decide as a group what is the spiciest and what is the blandest dish on the menu. What would Jesus order?

Write down all of the words you can remember to "It's Not Easy Being Green." Come up with an analogy for "being green" that applies to life today. When have you ever felt like that?

SCRIPTURE MENU

Have someone look up the verses, and ask the questions aloud.

1 Samuel 16:7
However, the Lord said to Samuel, "Do not consider his appearance or his height, for I have rejected him. The Lord does not look at the things man looks at. Man looks at the outward appearance, but the Lord looks at the heart."

Do you think God has a "point system"?

What are the job requirements here? Do you get vacation?

Proverbs 11:2 (MsgB)
The stuck-up fall flat on their faces,
   but down-to-earth people stand firm.

When was the last time you should have just kept your mouth shut?

Proverbs 15:13 (NIV)
A happy heart makes the face cheerful,
   but heartache crushes the spirit.

What does "garbage in, garbage out" mean? Is it true? Is it inevitable?

Matthew 5:13 (NIV)
"You are the salt of the earth. But if the salt loses its saltiness, how can it be made salty again? It is no longer good for anything, except to be thrown out and trampled by men."

If life is not what it should be, why are we so ready to blame God?

Does it seem like there are some people who get all the flavor life has to offer and some who just get a stick of gum? Is it real or is it just our perception when we're the ones with the Juicy Fruit™?

Read Romans 5:1–11 (NRSV).

Imagine that the biggest package on the delivery truck has your name on it. But there is no door handle on the outside of your house. Keep this analogy going. How does the driver know that you're home? How do you get the package inside?

Philippians 2:12–15 (The MsgB)

12 **What I'm getting at, friends, is that you should simply keep on doing what you've done from the beginning. When I was living among you, you lived in responsive obedience. Now that I'm separated from you, keep it up. Better yet, redouble your efforts. Be energetic in your life of salvation, reverent and sensitive before God.** 13 **That energy is** *God's* **energy, an energy deep within you, God...willing and working at what will give [God] the most pleasure.**

14 **Do everything readily and cheerfully—no bickering, no second-guessing allowed!** 15 **Go out into the world uncorrupted, a breath of fresh air in this squalid and polluted society. Provide people with a glimpse of good living and of the living God. Carry the light-giving Message into the night. . . .**

We can spend all day being cheerful and kind and at the end of the day someone will still pee in our Fruit Loops.™ So how is the verse above true?

Take Home Bag

Read Psalm 77.
Now go back to the place where you drew the line between you and God. Erase the line and draw it around the dot.

"You may as well like yourself. Just think of how much time
   you're going to have to spend with you."

—Jerry Lewis, in *The Nutty Professor*

SIGNATURE OF PARENT OR GUARDIAN

THEME: PARENTS

ORDER HERE

Whether you want to acknowledge it or not, your parents are probably the greatest influence on who you are right now. You can choose what to do about that influence, but you can't deny it exists. It is amazing how many people will blame their mom or dad for all the things they do not like about themselves but never give them credit for the things they do like about themselves! Your parents are a veritable library of information; in comparison, right now you are still only a notebook with a few pages of notes and doodles. Shouldn't you take advantage of the opportunity?

START THINKING

True of False?

- In real life, there is no such thing as a "Huxtable" house.
- If God didn't use the "Father" analogy, he'd get a whole lot more followers.
- The perfect age to become a parent is about 24. (Say if you think it's higher or lower).
- I am filled with the fear of heredity.
- I wish I knew my grandparents better.

TABLE NOTES

Using the blank spaces or the back of the menu or napkin, finish these thoughts.

● One thing I will never say to my own children is . . .

● If I could ask my grandparents one question about my mom/dad it would be...

Make a simple line drawing of each person in your household (you can include extended family). Keep it as simple as possible. Now go back and draw one detail on each person based on who that person is.

SCRIPTURE MENU

Look up one or more of the sets of verses, and respond to the discussion suggestions that follow.

Read Psalm 133:1–3.

When families get along, it's like...(Insert your own analogy.)

Read Psalm 143:1–12.

Dad knows how to read the map.

Read the following passages from Proverbs:

Proverbs 2:3–6

Proverbs 4:3

Proverbs 21:5-6

Proverbs 23:13–15

For each passage, write a "Mom-ism" or a "Dad-ism" in your own words.

TAKE HOME BAG

Find a time when your hands are busy (cooking dinner, washing the car), and ask your mother or father what was the hardest part about being a teenager.

TIP

Your children will look at you with the exact same "face" with which you look at your parents.

I AM WHAT I AM

THEME: INTEGRITY

ORDER HERE

Integrity means the kind of person you are when no one is looking.

Read that sentence again. Make sure you fully understand the concept. Give yourself a moment to think about it and then move on.

START THINKING

True or False?

- If the clerk gives me too much change and I notice before I leave the line, I would give it back.
- If the clerk gives me too much change and I don't notice until I'm in my car, I would give it back.
- If I found a wallet, I would turn it in to lost and found, but I would probably keep the money.
- If I could get a guaranteed B on a test and not have to study, I would still study and go for the A.
- I've never parked in the handicapped spot.
- I've never used the handicapped bathroom stall.

TABLE NOTES

Here's an oldie but goodie. Take a five-dollar bill. Choose one of the scripture verses from Proverbs, and write it on the back of the bill. Tear out a sheet of paper from your journal or write on the back of a place mat, "Jeremy, Here's the five bucks I owe you." Tack both the bill and the note to the community bulletin board in the shop. Sit back and see what happens. (Do **NOT** confront someone who takes the money.)

Choose three or four of the Proverb verses from the Scripture Menu and write them in your journal or on the back of a place mat. See if you can sum up, or condense, each into less than five words.

SCRIPTURE MENU

Have someone look up the verses, and ask the questions aloud.

Leviticus 19:11 (The MsgB)
"Don't steal.
"Don't lie.
"Don't deceive anyone."

It doesn't get much plainer than that, and yet we find a way to complicate the simplest things. Do we put conditions on what we consider "stealing"? Stealing a car is a crime. Is stealing a pack of gum? Have you ever stolen anything? A grade? A test answer? Ever walked out of a restaurant without paying? Why would some people have no problem with "little thefts"?

Read Psalm 25.

David didn't have a huge track record when it came to the whole integrity thing. Why would God choose someone who isn't perfect?

Read Luke 8:4–8.

How deep are your roots? How do you know?

Read Luke 16:1–12.

Does this seem true to you? Does it seem like the ones who lie, cheat, and steal are the ones who get ahead? How do you keep from simply "joining the cheaters"?

Titus 3:8 (MsgB)
You can count on this. I want you to put your foot down. Take a firm stand on these matters so that those who have put their trust in God will concentrate on the essentials that are good for everyone.

Have you ever confronted someone you caught cheating? What happened?

TAKE HOME BAG

Read Proverbs 21:16–31.

Choose just one verse that seems to speak to your life as it is right now. Write it down in your journal or on the back of the place mat. Commit it to memory before the next gathering.

TIP

Don't ever think that no one is looking.

MODEL BEHAVIOR

THEME:
ROLE MODELS

ORDER HERE

We all have heroes and role models. We may not even be aware of some of these ourselves. Other times we make a conscious effort to figure out exactly who we admire. Role models are important, but so is individuality. Having heroes is important but so is understanding their humanity. We are all teachers AND students, workers AND managers, builders AND bulldozers. If you think of yourself as an empty glass and fill yourself with other people, you don't have room for you. Role models and heroes are the flavor that gets spooned in to make you better at being you.

START THINKING

Choose the most appropriate option.

- I am more like Charlie Brown / Snoopy.
- I am the bass player / the lead singer.
- I am the coffee / the cream and sugar.
- I want to change the world / change the station.
- I am a violin playing a concerto / an I-Pod playing "I Like Big Butts."
- I am the monkey bars / the swings / the seesaw.

TABLE NOTES

Use the blank spaces or the back of the menu or napkin...

● Write down the name of your childhood hero.

● Write down the name of whoever is your hero now.

● Write down two or three names (from fiction or history) of people you greatly admire.

● Take all your answers and write down the things they have in common.

SCRIPTURE MENU

Look up one or more of the sets of verses, and respond to the discussion suggestions that follow.

2 Corinthians 9:10 (The New Testament and Psalms: An Inclusive Version)
Now the one who supplies seed to the sower and bread for food will also supply and increase your store of seed and will enlarge the harvest of your righteousness.

Are we really all part of one process? Is everything in this world connected to everything else in one way or another?

Is this a legitimate "real world" way of seeing things? Why or why not?

What if you choose to live your life this way?

What is the "harvest of YOUR righteousness"?

What do you produce in abundance that you can share with everyone else?

Ephesians 4:23-24 (The New Testament and Psalms: An Inclusive Version)
²³ **Be made new in the attitude of your minds;** ²⁴ **and...put on the new self, created to be like God in true righteousness and holiness.**

Is God the ultimate role model? Is it even reasonable to think such a thing?

What would happen if someone asked you who your role model is and you said, "God"?

Part of wisely choosing a role model is acknowledging her/his faults. How can you do that with God as your role model?

1 Timothy 4:12 (NIV)
Don't let anyone look down on you because you are young, but set an example for the believers in speech, in life, in love, in faith, and in purity.

Is there such a thing as role model responsibility?

Read the verse and give some "real world" ideas on how you

can be a role model for so-called adults who hover around your life.

Proverbs 22:6 (NRSV)
Train children in the right way,
and when old, they will not stray.

In Exploration 6 we thought about our parents and their authority. One of the scariest parts about being a parent is that you realize you are a role model twenty-four hours a day. List a few ways you are like one or the other of your parents.

Is this a learned behavior? How much of who you are is heredity?

Is there anything your parents do that you have already decided, "I'll never do that to my kids"?

Philippians 3:17 (NRSV)
Brothers and sisters, join in imitating me, and observe those who
live according to the example you have in us.

Who is your role model?

Basketball great Charles Barkley once said, "I am not a role model." When it comes down to it, in what ways do we or don't we have a choice?

TAKE HOME BAG

Read Psalm 101.

There are at least ten ways that David says he is a role model. How many can you apply to yourself? *Write down the names of people that see you as a role model.*

That whole "you are the only Jesus that some people will ever see" thing—that's true. Scary, isn't it?

GOOOO AAAAALLLL!

THEME: GOALS + DREAMS

ORDER HERE

Genesis chapter 37 says, "And Joseph dreamed a dream." It is an amazing verse if you read it in the context of the whole story. Joseph is the little daddy's boy who is a pain to his brothers. Yet Joseph has this dream in which the universe itself is bowing down to him. The problem was that Joseph could not accomplish that dream being the "Joseph" that he was then. He had to go through hell and become an entirely different "Joseph" in order to realize that goal.

START THINKING

Take money, location, and education out of the equation, and then complete these thoughts.

- If I could be anything I wanted when I am an adult, I would be...

- If I could live anywhere in the world I would live...

- If I could drop everything right now and just "go," I would go to...

- If I could change the world in one way, I would...

- Before this day is over, I want to...

True or False?

- It is possible to dream too large.
- It is possible to dream too small.

TABLE NOTES

Use the place mat or napkin...

● Draw a picture of your face, and then add a little "thought balloon," like in the comics.

● Inside the thought balloon draw a picture or a word that represents a dream that you have always had.

● Fold the place mat or napkin into a football. Have someone else at the table make "finger goal posts." See who can get the most "goals" in just five tries each.

If you shared your dreams with others, who would be the most likely to try to squash your dreams?

Who would be the most likely to support you?

SCRIPTURE MENU

Have someone look up the verses, and ask the questions aloud.

Philippians 3:12-20 (MsgB)

¹² I'm not saying that I have this all together, that I have it made. But I am well on my way, reaching out for Christ, who has so wondrously reached out for me. ¹³ Friends, don't get me wrong: By no means do I count myself an expert in all of this, but I've got my eye on the goal, where God is beckoning us onward—to Jesus. ¹⁴ I'm off and running, and I'm not turning back.

¹⁵ So let's keep focused on that goal, those of us who want everything God has for us. If any of you have something else in mind, something less than total commitment, God will clear your blurred vision—you'll see it yet! ¹⁶ Now that we're on the right track, let's stay on it.

¹⁷ Stick with me, friends. Keep track of those you see running this same course, headed for this same goal. ¹⁸ There are many out there taking other paths, choosing other goals, and trying to get you to go along with them. I've warned you of them many times; sadly, I'm having to do it again. All they want is easy street. They hate Christ's Cross. ¹⁹ But easy street is a dead-end street. Those who live there make their bellies their gods; belches are their praise; all they can think of is their appetites.

²⁰ But there's far more to life for us. We're citizens of high heaven! We're waiting the arrival of the Savior, the Master, Jesus Christ....

What does "Eyes on the Prize" mean? Can you think of an example from history or your own life?

James 4:13-15 (NIV)

¹³ Now listen, you who say, "Today or tomorrow we will go to this or that city, spend a year there, carry on business and make money." ¹⁴ Why, you do not even know what will happen tomorrow. What is your life? You are a mist that appears for a little while and then vanishes. ¹⁵ Instead, you ought to say, "If it is the Lord's will, we will live and do this or that."

Do we dream too much? Is that possible? What are the consequences of "living for today"?

Proverbs 15:22 (NIV)
Plans fail for lack of counsel,
but with many advisers they succeed.

Proverbs 21:5 (NIV)
The plans of the diligent lead to profit
as surely as haste leads to poverty.

These two verses from Proverbs are similar but offer two different pieces of advice for making your goals come true. What is the advice?

Jeremiah 18:1–6 (NIV)
¹This is the word that came to Jeremiah from the Lord: ²"Go down to the potter's house, and there I will give you my message." ³So I went down to the potter's house, and I saw him working at the wheel. ⁴But the pot he was shaping from the clay was marred in his hands; so the potter formed it into another pot, shaping it as seemed best to him.

⁵Then the word of the Lord came to me: ⁶"O house of Israel, can I not do with you as this potter does?" declares the Lord. "Like clay in the hand of the potter, so are you in my hand, O house of Israel."

If God is the potter and we are the clay, what is the fire? Is your "fire" different than everyone else's? How would God "use the pieces" to make a new pot?

Romans 9:21 (NIV)
Does not the potter have the right to make out of the same lump of clay some pottery for noble purposes and some for common use?

Which "vessel" is closest to your life? Why?

Matthew 6:33 (The New Testament and Psalms: An Inclusive-Version)

But strive first for the dominion of god and god's righteousness, and all these things will be given to you as well.

God gave you those dreams to begin with. How easy (difficult) is patience when it comes to realizing your dreams? Explain.

Take Home Bag

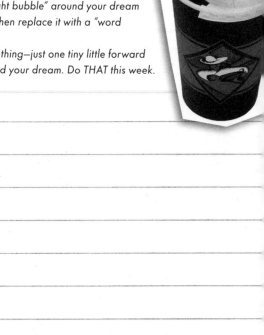

Read 2 Thessalonians 2:15–17.
Erase the "thought bubble" around your dream on your paper, then replace it with a "word bubble."
Write down one thing—just one tiny little forward movement toward your dream. Do THAT this week.

Tip

If you can accomplish your dream by being everything that you are right now, then your dream is too small.

♪ DES-TA-NEEE, DES-TA-NEEE- NO ESCAPING THAT FOR ME*

THEME: DESTINY

ORDER HERE

The word for "destiny," or "predestined," occurs six times in the scriptures (see Scripture Menu). Do you believe that God has life all laid out? Do you believe in chance? Some people say, "It's my destiny to..." and then fill it in with whatever they want.

Sometimes we don't see destiny for what it is until after it's already been accomplished. One thing we can be sure of is that God has a plan. Whether or not God decides to share it with us is up for interpretation.

START THINKING

True or False?

- God knows what my great-grandchild will name her pet cat.
- God has already chosen who I'm going to marry.
- Nothing happens without God's approval.

*Gene Wilder in the movie Young Frankenstein (1974)

- God knew I was going to make the last stupid decision I made and let me make it for a reason.
- God made the earth, hung it in space, gave it a spin, and only occasionally checks in to see how things are going.
- God gave us a path, but we can choose to stay on or wander off it.
- God's plan for my life constantly changes based on my actions.
- God put everyone in my life for a reason.

TABLE NOTES

Write down three great moments in history as well as something you did this morning.

Check out these verses:

Exodus 3:14
John 1:1
Revelations 1:8
Revelation 10:5-6

Some theorize that God lives in an "eternal now." With God there is no past, present, or future—only now. That would mean that to God, those four things you wrote down are all happening "now."

SCRIPTURE MENU

Have someone look up the verses, and ask the questions aloud.

Acts 4:27-28 (MsgB)

27 "For in fact they did meet—Herod and Pontius Pilate with nations and peoples, even Israel itself!—met in this very city to plot against your holy Son Jesus, the One you made Messiah, 28 to carry out the plans you long ago set in motion."

What would be an example of something God set in motion that we must "carry out"?

Romans 8:29-30 (The New Testament and Psalms: An Inclusive Version)

29 For those whom God foreknew were also predestined to be conformed to the image of God's Child, in order that Christ might be the firstborn within a large family. 30 And those whom god predestined God also called; and those whom God called God also justified; and those whom God justified God also glorified.

If you don't believe in God, can you still believe in destiny?

1 Corinthians 2:7 (The New Testament and Psalms: An Inclusive Version)

But we speak God's wisdom, secret and hidden, which God decreed before the ages for our glory.

Have you ever gone through something and then years later figured out, "Oh, that's why?" Talk about that for a moment.

Ephesians 1:5 (The New Testament and Psalms: An Inclusive Version)

God destined us for adoption as God's children through Jesus Christ, according to the good pleasure of God's will.

Every family has a "black sheep." Is it possible that we were the "black sheep" of God's family, so God sent Jesus as a "shepherd"?

Ephesians 1:11 (MsgB)
It's in Christ that we find out who we are and what we are living for. Long before we first heard of Christ and got our hopes up, he had his eye on us, had designs on us for glorious living.

Where do you think Christianity will be in a thousand years?

TAKE HOME BAG

Tear a small piece off your place mat or a piece of paper. Tuck this into the frame of your bedroom mirror or in your wallet. Read Psalm 16. Remember that when we look at our lives we see only the one small piece. God is looking at the entire picture.

TIP

If you keep looking over your shoulder at the past, your future is going to be an oncoming train.

WHOOOO ARE YOU? WHO? WHO?

THEME:
SELF-IMAGE/ SELF-ESTEEM

ORDER HERE

Most people have at least a slight self-image problem. Don't think that's true? How many advertisers make a nice sale off the idea that you could be so much more IF you just used a particular product? You could be cool. The problem the Pharisees (know-it-alls) had with Jesus was that not only did Jesus not *want* to hang out with them but Jesus also actually *preferred* to hang out with the outcasts. The idea that you must be someone else in order to be accepted too often translates into our religion. For centuries people have been turned away from God's house because of who they are. People sometimes act in very un-Christ like ways in the name of Christ.

START THINKING

Complete each sentence.

● The Ben & Jerry's flavor that is most like me is...

● The item on the menu that represents my emotional state today is...

● The part of a car that best describes me is...

● If I had to wear a picture of Jesus on my T-shirt, it would be...

● The worst thing anyone's ever said to me was...

● The worst thing I ever said about myself was...

● If I could change one thing about me it would be...

TABLE NOTES

Make two columns in your book or on the back of a place mat. One column is called Respected the other column is called Rejected.

● List five people in each column; these can include celebrities.

● Add your name to one list or the other. Add Jesus' name.

● Separately from the group, write down the name of someone you know in school or in church who is completely comfortable with who she/he is and doesn't give a rat's butt what other people think.

SCRIPTURE MENU

Look up one or more sets of verses as a group and respond to the discussion suggestions that follow.

Read Psalm 145:1–21 (MsgB).
Read Mark 4:26–28.

Talk about a time when you pulled a big idea out of your past to help you in your present.

Read Romans 2:1.

Is there a "Christian" version of karma?

Read Ephesians 4:12–16.

Jesus is not easy. Can you think of a time when you or a friend had to defend yourselves for what you believed? Talk about it.

Read James 3:13–17.

How do you live your faith? Have you ever been told you don't do it right? What is your response? What does this verse say about those who point their fingers?

Read James 5:13–16.

When and how do you usually pray? In what ways could prayer be an action?

TAKE HOME BAG

Read Psalm 118.
In the columns you made for Table Notes, erase any names you wrote under Rejected and put them under Respected.

TIP

God has never once said, "Oops." Not ever.

FROM THE INSIDE OUT

Theme: BEING PURE IN HEART

Order Here

In Jesus' time it was believed that different aspects of life were controlled by different areas of the body. The heart was the center of all things. It was the place of the soul. When we think of "being pure" or "living pure," we usually think of the perfect people in the perfect house in the perfect neighborhood. They don't really exist. That's an unrealistic expectation. Living with a pure heart simply means that we make the choice to live our lives putting others ahead of ourselves. We genuinely go out of our way to seek a closer relationship with God by our actions, not just our words. Living in a constant state of complaining and arguing creates plaque on the heart. Living with a pure heart means getting rid of the plaque.

Start Thinking

Attitude adjustment: Write down a number between 1 and 10 that shows which "attitude" is closer to the way you live.

1 ——————————— 10

Look at the Autumn Leaves...

I bet if you ran into that tree hard enough, it would kill you.

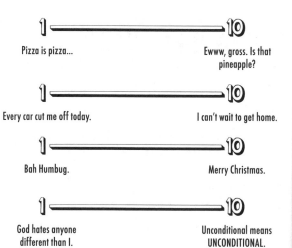

1 —————————— 10

Pizza is pizza...

Ewww, gross. Is that pineapple?

1 —————————— 10

Every car cut me off today.

I can't wait to get home.

1 —————————— 10

Bah Humbug.

Merry Christmas.

1 —————————— 10

God hates anyone different than I.

Unconditional means UNCONDITIONAL.

TABLE NOTES

In your book or on the back of a place mat, draw a picture of a wall. Use multiple "bricks" to "build" it. Near the wall make a list of words that suggest ways to live with your heart pure (not perfect). You can list mature decisions you've made or things you've done that are unselfish. Think about times when you've been open to ideas other than your own. For each word you come up with, erase a brick from your wall.

God is right beside us all the time. It is when we make the choice to live with "pure hearts" that we can finally see the God who has been there all the time.

Scripture Menu

Look up one or more of the sets of verses, and respond to the discussion suggestions that follow.

Read Matthew 5:8.

Jesus draws a distinction between living IN the world and being OF the world. What is the difference in your life?

Read 1 Timothy 1:5.

Who would be the last person you'd want to see in heaven?

Why would it bother you to be seated next to them at the Welcome to Heaven party?

Read 2 Timothy 2:22.

Name some people you know who you think have a pure heart. What is it about them that you admire? In what ways do you see those traits in yourself? If you don't see them, how can you fix that?

Take Home Bag

Years ago homeless men called hobos (short for *homeward bound*) would ride the trains and get off at various neighborhoods to beg a meal from local houses. They would often use something called the "hobo alphabet" to mark the curb in front of a house to let others who were riding the rails know that this was a place to get a meal. These marks looked something like this:

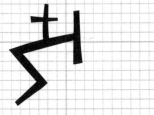

Read Psalm 51.

Imagine you could actually put a tattoo on your heart. Create your own symbol that would say "Good place to get help."

Being a Christian isn't about being perfect. It's about one beggar showing another beggar where the bread is.

ARE YOU OUT OF YOUR MIND?

THEME: BEING AUDACIOUS

ORDER HERE

Audaciousness is that little thing that flits through your brain that tells you that you can do something totally crazy and completely at odds with all other forms of logic. Have you ever watched people on the Web doing something called "parkour" or "freerunning"? We watch people do these jaw-dropping moves and think, "These guys are out of their freaking minds." What if we could say that when we watch someone be a Christian? How could you astound someone watching you at work? What would that kind of "servanthood" look like?

START THINKING

Choose one of each.

● Breakfast means:

Plain bagel / Everything bagel with jalapeno cream cheese

● Swimming means:

Dipping your toes in the shallow end first / High Dive—Cannonball—3, 2, 1

- Food drive means:

Door-to-door can goods collecting / Sitting outside corporate offices until they agree to underwrite the soup kitchen for a year

- Bible study means:

1 Corinthians 13 with donuts / Judges with Red Bull

- Communion means:

Wonder Bread and Welch's / Consecrated Fruit Loops™ & chocolate milk

- Worship means:

Stained glass and hymns / Build your own altar out of trash at a truck stop and invite the drivers to join you

TABLE NOTES

Choose one of the scripture verses from the Scripture Menu that speaks to you. Write it down on a piece of paper or on the back of a place mat. Ask God to send God's word to someone who really needs to hear it today. Now fold the paper into an airplane and fly it across the coffee shop, or stick it under someone's windshield.

SCRIPTURE MENU

Have someone look up the verses, and ask the questions aloud.

Read Luke 5:17–20.

In Jesus' time there was only one person who was allowed to read the verse that Jesus reads here. That would be the Messiah. Imagine if you stood up and touched or even broke the most sacred thing in your church and said, "It's okay, folks. I'm God."

Read Matthew 14:28–31.

What would it take to make the decision to take that first step out of the boat? Seriously: What would it take to make you defy all logic?

Read John 6:60–69.

Don't look at the previous verses. Just read these few. Whenever Jesus thought followers were just in it for the grins he pulled out the hard stuff. What is the hardest lesson (biblical or otherwise) that you have had to learn?

Read Job 8:21.

Why do we think we're supposed to be quiet in church?

Read Proverbs 20:11.

For which of these would you get in more trouble? Why?

- Wearing a T-shirt with a picture of Jesus on a skateboard
- Wearing a T-shirt with a picture of the President in his underwear

Read Philippians 3:7–10.

Who gets to decide what is "proper" when it comes to religion?

TAKE HOME BAG

Read Psalm 58.
Rewrite the psalm as if it were the lyrics of a
Green Day or Sex Pistols song.

_____
_____
_____
_____
_____
_____
_____
_____
_____
_____
_____
_____

Think of one thing you do for God in a given month. Just one.
Now imagine what you would have to do to make that an
"audacious" thing for God.
Now Do That.

Are you the hammer or the nail?

WABBIT SEASON! DUCK SEASON!

Theme: CONFLICT

Order Here

Conflict has always been with us. Since Cain made his point with Abel we seem to have been at one another's throats. What's the first card game many of us learn to play? War.

Do you remember the old Looney Toon cartoons? Bugs and Daffy go back and forth, back and forth, until somebody gets shot. Usually our own conflicts are more like Bugs and Elmer in "Rabbit of Seville." Bugs chases Elmer with a razor. Elmer chases Bugs with a hatchet. Bugs chases Elmer with an ax. Elmer chases Bugs with a pistol. Bugs chases Elmer with a canon. And so on and so on. Conflicts have a tendency to escalate. It's how we deal with them that shows our true character. In the 1982 cold war movie *War Games*, a young computer hacker teaches a computer how to play a game called Global Thermal Nuclear War, and it's the computer that finally decides: "A silly game, the only way to win is not to play."

Start Thinking

True or False?

- I am calm under pressure.
- I will argue to find a solution more than I will to win the argument.
- Sometimes it is necessary to argue with people to find out what they really think.
- Solving a conflict is rarely about who gets loudest.
- I have no problem telling authority figures that I disagree with them.

- The ultimate goal in any relationship (personal or between nations) is peace.
- Might makes right.
- Sometimes God chooses sides.

TABLE NOTES

Draw a stick figure in the center of a blank page or on the back of a place mat. This figure represents you. Draw several other items on the page, with the distance you put between the item and the stick figure representing how much "conflict" there is between you. The more distance between the item and the stick figure, the greater the conflict. Ready?

- Draw mom.
- Draw dad.
- Draw a school.
- Draw something that represents your future.
- Draw a cross (God/Jesus). (It's perfectly okay to feel conflict here. Lots of great Bible folks did.)
- Draw a church.
- Draw something that represents the current U.S. administration.

SCRIPTURE MENU

Have someone look up the verses, and ask the questions aloud.

Read Ezekiel 22:30.

The "wall" here is an analogy for faithful people. What do you think this verse is saying? How could it apply to the church to-day?

Read Romans 12:4–5.

Fighting with a friend or family member is like the hand fighting with the knee. Think about the last conflict you had that no-body won (in the long run). Is a victory in the short run worth it? How?

Read James 3:13–4:2.

James mentions "good fruit" in this verse. Check out Galatians 5:22–23 for what is meant by "good fruit." Now think about the last big conflict you had. What might have happened if you had used any of the "good fruits"?

TAKE HOME BAG

Look at these verses from Proverbs.

Proverbs 12:20
Proverbs 15:1
Proverbs 16:17–22

Choose three verses and decide which verse fits with the conflict drawings you have in your journal or on the place mat. Find a way to apply that verse this week.

Tip

It takes two to tango.

HINDSIGHT 20/20

Theme: THE PAST

Order Here

There's a wonderful moment in the Disney movie *The Lion King* when wise old Rafiki bonks Simba on the head with his staff. Simba says, "What was that for?" Rafiki responds, "It doesn't matter. It's in the past." Simba protests. "Yeah, but it still hurts." A consoling Rafiki says, "Oh yes, the past can hurt but the way I see it you can either run from it, or learrrrrrn from it."

Start Thinking

Complete each thought.

● The best toy I ever got as a gift was...

● The toy I always wanted and didn't get was...

● The best teacher I ever had was...

● The earliest memory I have of my father is...

● The earliest memory I have of my mother is...

● The first Christmas play I was in, my role was...

● The first time I can remember that God was more than a word to me
   was...

TABLE NOTES

Draw a line from one end of your paper to the other, Using a blank page in your journal or the back of a place mat. Make a time line with the five greatest moments of your life. Now go back and write in the five worst moments of your life. Now look at the time line and mark the times in your life when you grew the most as a person.

SCRIPTURE MENU

Look up one or more of the sets of verses, and respond to the discussion suggestions that follow.

Read 1 Corinthians. 10:11.

Is it true that those who don't learn from the past are condemned to repeat it? Can you think of a global or national example? Can you think of a personal example?

Read Job 8:8–10.

If you could go back in time and meet your grandparents when they were your age, what would you ask them? Can you think of something that we've "lost to the ages"?

Read Matthew 1:1–17.

Jesus' family tree includes both women who dressed as prostitutes and actual prostitutes, as well as various teachers, preachers, dancers, adulterers, and killers. How far back in your family can you recite? Do you think we place the same importance on our family trees today? Explain.

TAKE HOME BAG

Search through some old photo albums and find the earliest school picture of yourself that you can. Use your journal or a separate piece of paper and write a letter to that kid. What are the most important things he or she is going to need to learn or know about?

TIP

If you drag your past around with you like baggage, you'll never get to where you're going.

TAKE ME

THEME: LEADERSHIP

ORDER HERE

Does it seem as if we are in a leadership vacuum? There is a certain amount of respect we throw toward our leaders (church, community, country), but are our hearts always in it? It seems as if one side of "the aisle" is always forming a committee to impeach even before a person becomes President. What kind of leadership is that? Do we send our leaders to Washington to express our positions (democracy), or do we entrust those whom we elect to have our best interest at heart and allow them to represent us (republic)?

In either case, we want those who lead to be able to take appropriate action in a timely manner. When we say, "There is no leadership," we are often speaking out of frustration because we feel nothing is happening regarding what we feel are the most pressing problems.

START THINKING

Choose one.

- I know all the hot trends. / I couldn't care less about what's hot.
- People think of me as a good listener. / People seek out my advice.
- Electing a class president is just a popularity contest. / Student leaders can get things done if given a chance.
- Politics is (mostly) a dirty business. / Politics is (mostly) an honorable profession.
- Respect must be earned. / Respect is something you give to everyone unless given a reason not to.

TABLE NOTES

Read these verses.

Psalm 72
2 Timothy 1:7
John 13:1-17

Make a Checklist for Leaders—ten to fifteen one-word items that signify leadership for you. How well do our leaders score? (Include the President, the mayor of your town, the leadership of your church, and yourself.)

SCRIPTURE MENU

Look up one or more of the sets of verses, and respond to the discussion suggestions that follow.

Read Proverbs 11:12.

It was President Theodore Roosevelt who said, "Speak softly and carry a big stick." Is this effective leadership? Reread the verse from Proverbs. Which leadership style do you think is most effective? Why?

Read Daniel 4:30–35.

Do you think God punishes leaders who don't lead according to God's ideas? Do you think God chooses who will lead? If so, how? Why would some people think it's part of God's plan that we have the U.S. administration we have now? What about other world leaders?

Read Malachi 2:7.

Someone once said, "The job of the clergy is to protect the questions." Are there certain things we don't need to know? Are there certain things (within the church) that we should just accept as a "mystery"? If so, what and why? Is there any difference between leadership and "Christian" leadership? If so, what is it? Should there be?

Read Hebrews 13:17–18.

Do you want to see your leaders as human or as flawless? Which gives you more comfort? Which is more likely to make you follow?

TAKE HOME BAG

Read these two verses from the book of James: 1:19 and 3:5–6.

Use the Internet and look up a quotation from a leader you respect. Write it down in your journal or on a slip of paper, and then stick it on the wall near where you do your homework.

If you are blindly following the leader, what's going to happen when the leader ducks?

CANNONBALL!

THEME: COMMIMENT

ORDER HERE

There is a moment of "no going back." When your feet leave the diving board; when you stand up in a room full of people to voice your opinion on something; when you stand in front of friends, family, and God and pledge your life to a person who is pledging her/his life to you—that's commitment, that's the moment of no going back. Any moment of commitment takes acknowledging the possibility of failure (Big Whopping Painful Failure and "Aw Shoot" failure). Commitment also takes faith, hope, belief, and the expectation that everything will be okay.

START THINKING

Which one of each pair is closer to the "you" that you are?

- Pass the ketchup. / Pass the hot sauce.
- Study every night. / What? There's a test today?
- Blueprints are art. / Gimme that big freakin' paint roller and stand back.
- Exactly 1/8 level teaspoon of baking powder, sifted. / How many chocolate chips in a fistful?

TABLE NOTES

In your journal or on the back of a place mat, draw a bird's eye view of a rectangular table. Draw six chairs (three on each side) and one chair at the head of the table. This is your Commitment Committee. Write your name at the head of the table, and then fill in the names of the other chairs as follows:

1. Risk Management Advisor—the realist in your life who will help you weigh the options
2. Encourager—the person you would most want behind you when it's time to jump out of the plane (metaphorically speaking)
3. The Voice of Experience—the most knowledgeable person you know who will give you all the background you need
4. The Bungee Jumper—the person who would be the most likely to strap himself/herself in with you just for the grins
5. The Wallet Holder—the person you would trust with all your valuables.
6. The Nay-Sayer—do *not* write in a name on this chair. Think about the person in your life who is most likely to kill your dreams, then *don't invite* that person to the table.

Scripture Menu

Have someone look up the verses, and ask the questions aloud.

Psalm 130:1–8 (TNCH)

A Song of Ascents.
1. **Out of the depths I cry to you, O God.**
2. **O god, hear my voice!**

Let your ears be attentive to the voice of my supplications!
³ If you, O God, should mark iniquities, who could stand?
⁴ But there is forgiveness with you, so that you may be revered.
⁵ I wait for God, my soul waits, and in God's word I hope;
⁶ my soul waits for God more than those who watch for the morning,
more than those who watch for the morning.
⁷ O Israel, hope in God!
For with God there is steadfast love.
With God is great power to redeem;
⁸ It is God who will redeem Israel form all its iniquities.

What was the biggest commitment you ever made to God? When did it happen? Have you ever prayed one of those on-your-knees-in-the-in-the-pouring-rain-screaming prayers? What happened after that?

Proverbs 17:17 (NIV)

A friend loves at all times,
and a brother is born for adversity.

This sounds like old-fashioned advice, but is it still true?

Proverbs 30:32 (NIV)

"If you have played the fool and exalted yourself,
or if you have planned evil,
clap your hand over your mouth!

Recall a few times when things happened to you as a result of your our own stupid behavior. How well do you take into the moment the repercussions of your actions?

Matthew 6:33 (The New Testament and Psalms: An Inclusive Version)

But strive first for the dominion of God and God's righteousness, and all these things will be given to you as well.

How much is God a part of your everyday decision making? Can you think of an example?

Read Matthew 14:28–36 (NIV).

What's the craziest thing you've ever done on a whim? Recall a time in your life when you thought it was best to put planning aside and just jump in and see what would happen. Do you know anyone who lives this way? How much of being a Christian is about preplanning and how much is about just stepping out of the boat?

1 Corinthians 13:13 (NIV)

And now these three remain: faith, hope and love. But the greatest of these is love.

Faith, hope, and love—which one is hardest for you to do?

Titus 2:7–9 (NIV)

[7] In everything set them an example by doing what is good. In your teaching show integrity, seriousness [8] and soundness of speech that cannot be condemned, so that those who oppose you may be ashamed because they have nothing bad to say about us.

[9] Teach slaves to be subject to their masters in everything, to try to please them, not to talk back to them...

This passage seems to be a list of guidelines for committing yourself to being a follower of Jesus. Can you think of one or two you'd add to this list based on our time and culture?

TAKE HOME BAG

Look at your Commitment Committee table again. Decide which chair you sit in at someone else's table. Sometime this week, send that person an e-mail or a note, or talk with the person and fulfill that role.

TIP

"Measure twice. Cut once."

—Bob Villa

FIND OUT WHAT IT MEANS TO ME

Theme: RESPECT

Order Here

In the 1991 movie *The Fisher King*, Robin Williams says, "You know, boys...there's three things in this world that you need: respect for all kinds of life, a nice bowel movement on a regular basis, and a navy blazer." Respect will show you a great deal about your character. How much do you show to others? How much do you show yourself? How much do you show to God?

Start Thinking

How true? Score the following statements on a Scale of Truthfulness, with 1 being Basically a Lie and 10 being Totally True.

● Celebrities should stop complaining about the paparazzi because they chose to be famous in the first place.

1 ═══════════════════════ 10

● Waiters and waitresses get paid to take your order and bring you your food. If they can't do it quick enough, then they don't get a tip.

1 ═══════════════════════ 10

● If I'm screwed up, it's my parents' fault.

1 ═══════════════════════ 10

- The President should be impeached.

1 ——————————————— 10

- The minister is here. Stop swearing.

1 ——————————————— 10

- You can't play the toilet-paper game in the sanctuary.

1 ——————————————— 10

- God is watching, and God's not happy.

1 ——————————————— 10

Table Notes

In the song "Respect," Aretha Franklin spells out the word—
"R-E-S-P-E-C-T." In the space below or on the back of a place
mat, write these letters in a vertical column. Come up with
a word for each letter of RESPECT that indicates a way you
can show respect to others, yourself, or God.

SCRIPTURE MENU

Look up one or more of the sets of verses, and respond to the discussion suggestions that follow.

Deuteronomy 30:4 (NIV)

Even if you have been banished to the most distant land under the heavens, from there our sovereign God will gather you and bring you back.

It's one of the most comforting verses in the whole book. What does it have to do with respect?

Read Proverbs 1:24–30 (NIV).

Determine whose voice the verse sounds like to you. Maybe someone from your own life?

Is it disrespectful to talk in the movie theater during the movie? Is it disrespectful to talk while the teacher is talking? Is it disrespectful to answer your cell phone when you're having lunch with someone? Explain.

1 Peter 2:17 (NIV)

Show proper respect to everyone: Love the brotherhood of believers, fear God, honor the king.

How do we show respect to our leaders? We can complain all we want, but when it comes down to it, how many of us could send troops into harm's way? Does power ultimately bring respect? Should it? Why or why not?

Joshua 24:15 (NIV)

"But if serving the Lord seems undesirable to you, then choose for yourselves this day whom you will serve, whether the gods your forefathers served beyond the River, or the gods of the Amorites, in whose land you are living. But as for me and my household, we will serve the Lord."

1 Samuel 16:7 (NRSV)

But the Lord said to Samuel, "Do not look on his appearance or on the height of his stature, because I have rejected him; for the Lord

does not see as mortals see; they look on the outward appearance, but the Lord looks on the heart."

Does it seem like the "pretty people" get all the respect? Is it respect or admiration? What is the difference? Is the person you respect the most one of the "pretty people"?

Proverbs 28:13 (NRSV)

No one who conceals transgressions will prosper,
but one who confesses and forsakes them will
obtain mercy.

Is it okay for our heroes to have flaws? Does that make a difference in how much we respect them? Give some examples.

Matthew 7:1 (NIV)

Do not judge, or you too will be judged.

Compare several translations of the verse from Matthew.

Read Galatians 6:2–6 (NRSV).

What is the difference between self-respect and egotism? When does one become the other?

Read Ephesians 4:22–25 (NRSV).

Does God respect us? If the old saying about "You are the only Jesus some people will ever see" is true, how should we respond? Do we have an obligation? How so?

Read Philippians 2:3–4 (NIV).

How do we earn respect? Think of someone you respect a great deal. How did that person obtain your respect?

Read Hebrews 12:14–16 and 1 Peter 4:7–8 (MsgBB).

Why is it so hard to respect some people? If God calls on us to love the way God does, are we in trouble? How can you love someone unconditionally and still respect that person?

TAKE HOME BAG

Look up these three passages.

Matthew 7:12 (Respect Each Other)
2 Timothy 2:15 (Respect God)
Genesis 1:26-31 (Respect the Earth)

Choose one of the passages on which to focus this week, and think of a way to fulfill it.

Imagine that every man woman and child on the planet has something to teach you. Imagine you have something to teach every man, woman, and child on the planet. We are all teachers. We are all students.

AFTERWORD:
HOW TO USE THIS BOOK

This book was born out of a conversation with a friend of mine at a large church in the central United States. She said that her church was going to do away with the traditional Sunday night meetings because of low attendance. They would keep Sunday morning as well as the Wednesday night Bible study. "The thing is," she said, "I still have fifty kids in and out of my office during the week, and it's not necessarily the same kids. What I need is a curriculum that requires no preparation—and that I can grab off my shelf, take four youth, and say 'Let's go over to Starbucks.'"

This book works two ways. The first is as an impromptu discussion starter to be used with five or less youth crammed into a booth at your favorite coffee shop or diner. The participants can write on place mats or napkins. Just you, a Bible (or a few, different versions), and a couple of pens, and you're ready to go.

You can also use this book as part of an on-going curriculum. If possible, give each participant his or her own copy of this book to write in and doodle on as a journal. If youth are sharing copies, it would be great if each youth could get his or her own journal, one that's small enough to fit into a book bag and be re-read or worked on at home.

Adapt It Up
Every youth worker has opened a book of games or discussions only to be faced with the first line, "Break your group into smaller groups of eight"—and you have a total of only six teens in the room. We've all had to "adapt it down" and try to make a large-group activity fit with a small group. This book is written so that a youth minister or Sunday school teacher can adapt it *up* for use with a larger group.

How to Use This Book
Each exploration is broken into six smaller sections. The activities can be followed sequentially or not.

Order Here
This is the introduction. You can read it aloud to your youth, or, if each has his or her own book, you can have them read along silently before moving on.

Start Thinking
These are quick focusing questions to get kids' brains in the proper mindset and the discussion moving. They are mostly fun questions, meant to start things off. There are no right or wrong answers, so pay attention to the responses. If possible, ask more questions based on the answers you receive. These answers will give you a good idea of where the discussion wants to go.

Table Notes

This section encourages active participation. Youth are asked to make lists, draw pictures, and so on. Make sure they know they don't have to be artists or poets to properly participate. Sometimes discussion is easier if your hands are busy, so encourage doodling—yes, in the books! The idea is to get teens to open up and talk about what they are thinking.

Scripture Menu

Encourage your youth to bring their own Bibles. Tell them they can go out and buy a translation that speaks to them (the more variety, the better). Be open to the idea of letting participants mark and write in their Bibles—to really use the books.

This section offers up several different scriptures. Use as many as you want. Each scripture reference is followed by one, two, or several discussion questions. This time may be when you have the deepest discussion and when participants may start asking their own questions. Pay attention to these and follow their logic—this book should be merely the starting point for deeper things. The goal is to help youth learn who they are and what they think and believe, and then to share that with others.

Take Home Bag

This section is a work-at-home assignment. If your participants each have their own books, this will be easier. If they don't, let them write down the assignment on the back of a place mat or napkin. If you are using this book as part of a regular gathering, tell participants that they don't have to share their answers unless they are comfortable doing so.

Tip

The tip is a quick "big idea" for the day, like a fortune in a cookie or the memorable quote on the side of the paper coffee cup. Encourage participants to see the tip as a life hint and to pay attention to how often it comes into play during the week.

The questions in this book have been around for ages. They are part of an attempt to explain our place in the universe. They are also questions that have inflamed many arguments and caused great schisms and separations in families and churches. It has been said that the job of the clergy is not to answer the questions but to protect them. Some things we won't know about God until we can pose the question face to face. In the meantime, this book is written to create discussion. If you don't come to a conclusion. . .just enjoy the ride.

Everyone likes to work with little kids. Their hugs are freely given, and they act like they are glad to see you. Finding leaders for the adult education program is a little harder, mostly because adults don't think they're smart enough to lead a Bible discussion. In adult classes you can have adult discussions, but you have chosen to work with teenagers. God bless you. I hope these books make you even better at what you do.